Brush With Greatness

# Rembrandt

Amie Jane Leavitt

PURPLE TOAD
PUBLISHING

PURPLE TOAD
PUBLISHING

Printing   1     2     3     4     5     6     7     8     9

Cézanne
Gainsborough
Goya
Leonardo da Vinci
Michelangelo

Monet
Rembrandt
Renoir
Van Gogh
Vermeer

**Publisher's Cataloging-in-Publication Data**
Leavitt, Amie Jane.
   Rembrandt / written by Amie Jane Leavitt.
      p. cm.
Includes bibliographic references, glossary, and index.
ISBN 9781624693236
eISBN 9781624693243
1. Rembrandt Harmenszoon van Rijn, 1606-1669—Juvenile literature. 2. Painters—Netherlands—Biography—Juvenile literature. I. Series: Brush with greatness.
 N6953.R4 2017
 759.9492
**Library of Congress Control Number:** 2016957439

**ABOUT THE AUTHOR:** Amie Jane Leavitt graduated from Brigham Young University. She has written more than sixty books for kids, has contributed to online and print media, and has worked for numerous educational publishing and assessment companies. To check out a listing of Amie's current projects and published works, visit her website at www.amiejaneleavitt.com.

**Previous page:** *The Polish Rider*, 1655

# Contents

Christ in the Storm on the Sea of Galilee, 1633

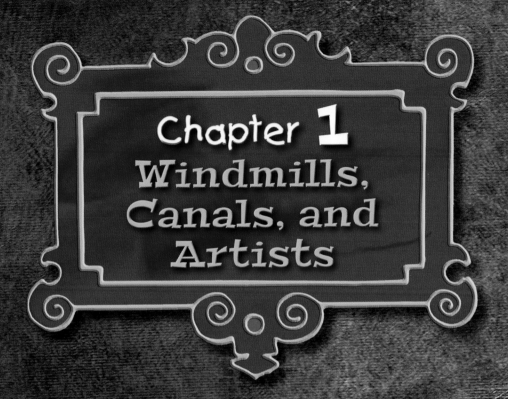

# Chapter 1
## Windmills, Canals, and Artists

Last night I dreamed about a painting I saw in an art gallery (GAL-uh-ree). In the painting, a stormy sea tosses a tall ship to and fro. The sailors try to keep the ship from flipping over.

I felt like I could swim right up to the ship and climb aboard. I could almost hear the crashing waves and smell the salty sea. The painting seemed so real, I even felt seasick.

The Mill, 1645–1648

All the way home, I couldn't stop thinking about the painting. And then it followed me into my dreams. The artist, Rembrandt, has painted many powerful works of art. He is also my teacher. I sure am lucky to be learning from this talented man!

I couldn't wait to get to art class today. It is my favorite day of the week. I walked quickly along the brick lane. Tall windmills line the street, like they do in many places in Holland. Their blades spin in slow circles when the wind blows. Small boats float in the canal (kuh-NAL) along the road. House lights sparkle on the water, twinkling like stars in the sky. Amsterdam is such a pretty place. No wonder such a famous artist lives here.

The Artist in His Studio, 1628

"Good morning, Mariska!" Rembrandt greets me as I walk into his studio. "You are here early today!" He is standing near his easel (**EE-zul**), which holds his latest masterpiece (**MAS-tur-peese**).

"What do you call this one?" I ask as I walk closer to the canvas (**KAN-vus**).

Rembrandt chuckles. "Can't you tell who this is?" He stands next to the painting, smiling.

Self-portraits

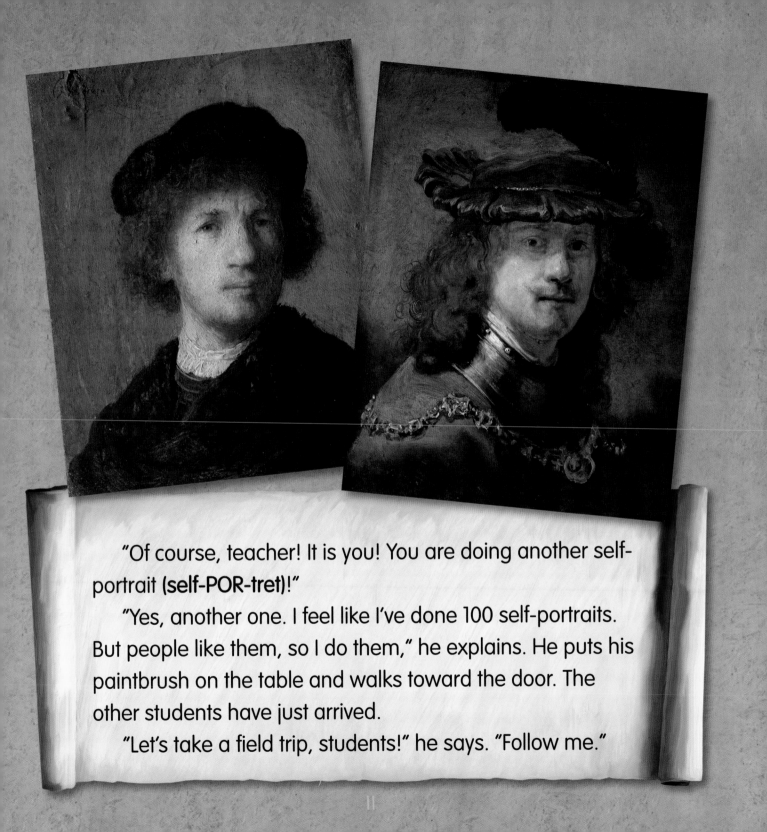

"Of course, teacher! It is you! You are doing another self-portrait (self-POR-tret)!"

"Yes, another one. I feel like I've done 100 self-portraits. But people like them, so I do them," he explains. He puts his paintbrush on the table and walks toward the door. The other students have just arrived.

"Let's take a field trip, students!" he says. "Follow me."

NETHERLANDS
(HOLLAND)

Groningen

AMSTERDAM

Leiden

Germany

Belgium

Rembrandt's home
in Leiden

# Chapter 2
# A Painter of Light

As we walk along the canal, Rembrandt tells us stories about his life as an artist. He grew up in Leiden, a town south of Amsterdam. It is also a land of windmills, brick streets, and canals. His father owned a windmill on the Rhine River.

Rembrandt was the youngest of nine children, but he still got to go to school. "I went to Latin school as a boy," he tells us now. "I learned a lot about the Bible and other important books there."

I picture some of his art in my mind. "Is this why you often paint Bible stories?"

"Yes, child," Rembrandt replies.

"I like your Bible paintings," Levi, my classmate, says. "My favorite is *The Parable [PAYR-uh-bul] of the Rich Fool*. The candle in the painting lights up everything that is important to the man. The way you painted it makes it look like a real light is shining on the painting. How do you do that?"

"Painting light isn't easy, Levi, but I will show you how to do it. I learned from my first art teacher, Jacob van Swanenburgh. He was a master painter of fire."

Rembrandt points to the canal. "Look at the way the sunlight flickers. It looks like a golden torch is in the water. Notice where you see light. Think about its color. Then you will know how to add it to your paintings."

The Parable of the
Rich Fool (1627)

The Night Watch
(1642)

## Chapter 3
## Watching the Night

We stroll to the end of the street. Rembrandt opens the door to the Musketeer **(mus-keh-TEER)** Meeting Hall. Several men tip their hats to greet us as we follow our teacher inside.

Rembrandt points to a huge painting in the grand hall. It stretches 12 feet across and more than 14 feet high. "This is my largest painting. It took me three years to finish," he explains. "I named it *The Night Watch*."

I can tell it is Rembrandt's artwork because of the light in the painting. He painted two men talking to each other. The moon is shining just on them. The other people in the painting are more in the shadows. One man in the corner holds a drum. Others are loading their muskets. It is clear that the men are getting ready for some kind of battle. There is a woman in the painting, too. I wonder where they are all going or what they are doing. Then I see a dog! I could stare at this painting for days and never see everything!

"I learned how to paint history like this from my second teacher," Rembrandt explains. "His name was Pieter Lastman. He is the reason I moved to Amsterdam. Good teachers are very important for artists," he says with a smile.

*Jonah and the Whale*
*by Pieter Lastman,*
*Rembrandt's teacher*

The Good Samaritan at the Inn (1633)

# Chapter 4
## More Than One Kind of Art

When we get back to the studio, Rembrandt asks us a question.

"Do artists only do one kind of art?" he asks.

"Some do, some don't," answers Anneke. "Which type are you, teacher?"

"You know that I paint," he says. "But did you know that I do etchings, too?"

I look around the room. All of my classmates have the same blank look I have. "What is an etching?" I finally ask.

"I'm so glad you asked, Mariska!" Rembrandt claps his hands with delight. "We will have our first lesson right now!"

(Left) The plate on which Rembrandt etched *Abraham Entertaining the Angels*. (Right) The print made from the etching.

Rembrandt opens a drawer and pulls out a pile of paper. They have pictures on them, made with black ink. "I didn't draw these on the paper," he explains. "I drew them on a metal plate covered in a type of wax. To make an etching, I use a needle to scrape a picture into the wax. Then I dip the plate in a special liquid. When I am done, I can use the metal plate to print many copies of my drawing."

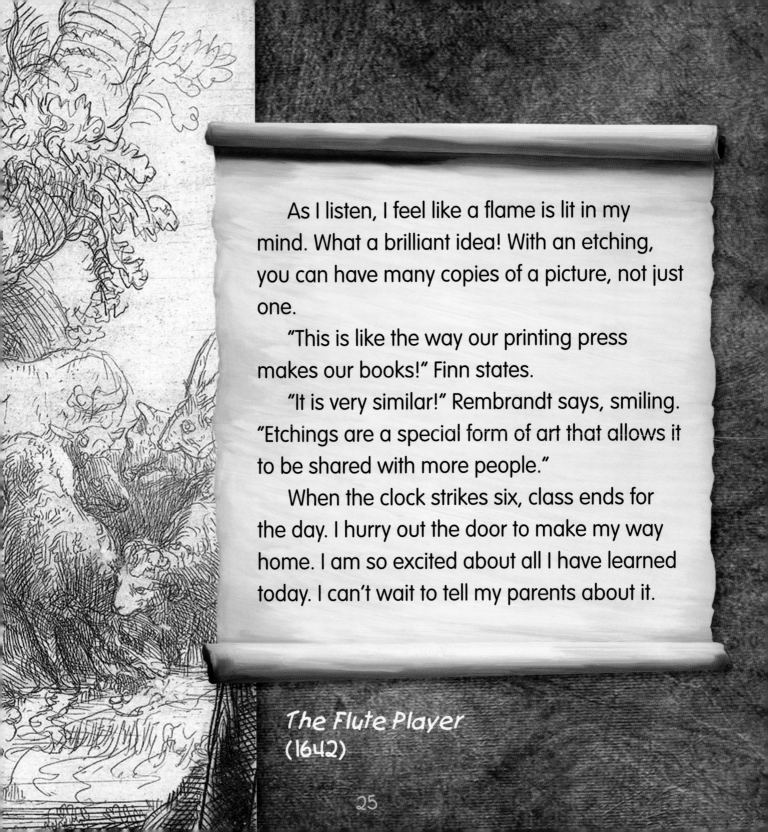

As I listen, I feel like a flame is lit in my mind. What a brilliant idea! With an etching, you can have many copies of a picture, not just one.

"This is like the way our printing press makes our books!" Finn states.

"It is very similar!" Rembrandt says, smiling. "Etchings are a special form of art that allows it to be shared with more people."

When the clock strikes six, class ends for the day. I hurry out the door to make my way home. I am so excited about all I have learned today. I can't wait to tell my parents about it.

*The Flute Player*
*(1642)*

The Sampling Officials (1662)

# Chapter 5
# An Artist's Life

At dinner, my parents ask me about art class. I tell them about visiting *The Night Watch* and learning how to etch. I promise to take them to the grand hall to show them *The Night Watch* on Saturday. They are excited to see it, too.

When I fall asleep, my dreams are sweet. I don't dream of sailing ships and rolling seas like I did last night. Instead I dream of drummers and men preparing for battle. And I dream of learning more about art from the famous Rembrandt. I can't wait to find out what we will learn tomorrow.

# Timeline

**1606**      Rembrandt Harmenszoon van Rijn is born in Leiden, The Netherlands, on July 15.

**1620**      He begins studying with Jacob van Swanenburgh.

**1624**      He spends six months studying with Pieter Lastman in Amsterdam, then sets up a studio in Leiden.

**1628**      He begins teaching art to his first students.

**1631**      He moves to Amsterdam permanently.

**1634**      He marries Saskia van Uylenburgh. They will have four children. Saskia is the model for many of his paintings.

**1639**      The family moves to a house in Amsterdam that becomes known as Rembrandt House.

**1642**      Saskia dies.

**1649**      Rembrandt meets his future wife, Hendrickje Stoffels. She becomes a model for him as well.

**1669**      Rembrandt dies on October 4. He is buried in Westerkerk, a church in Amsterdam.

## Paintings

## Etchings

*The Three Singers* (1624)

## Further Reading

### Works Consulted

"The Complete Life of the Painter Rembrandt van Rijn," *YouTube.com*. Retrieved July 15, 2016. https://www.youtube.com/watch?v=2r-LKEdR9zs

Dickey, Stephanie. "Rembrandt at 400." *Smithsonian Magazine*. December 2006. Retrieved July 15, 2016. http://www.smithsonianmag.com/arts-culture/rembrandt-at-400-138954962/?no-ist

"Rembrandt Born, July 15, 1606." *History.com*. Retrieved July 15, 2016. http://www.history.com/this-day-in-history/rembrandt-born

"Rembrandt, 1606–1669." *National Gallery*. Retrieved July 15, 2016. https://www.nationalgallery.org.uk/artists/rembrandt

"Rembrandt van Rijn (1606–1669): Paintings." *The Met*. Retrieved July 15, 2016. http://www.metmuseum.org/toah/hd/rmbt/hd_rmbt.htm

### Books

Cesar, Stanley. *Twenty-Four Rembrandt's Paintings (Collection) for Kids*. Amazon Digital Services, 2013.

Krull, Kathleen, and Kathryn Hewitt. *Lives of the Artists: Masterpieces, Messes (and What the Neighbors Thought)*. New York: Harcourt Brace & Company, 2014.

Spence, David. *Rembrandt (Essential Artists)*. London, England: Ticktock Books, 2009.

Spremulli, Paul. *Artist Masters for Kids: Rembrandt*. Coventry, RI: Angelnook Publishing, 2014.

Venezia, Mike. *Rembrandt (Getting to Know the World's Greatest Artists)*. New York: Scholastic, 2015.

### On the Internet

Rembrandt House Museum
http://www.rembrandthuis.nl/

Rembrandt van Rijn
http://www.rembrandtpainting.net/

**canal** (kuh-NAL)—A manmade ditch that is used to move boats and water from place to place.

**canvas** (KAN-vus)—Blank fabric on which artists paint.

**easel** (EE-zul)—A stand or frame that holds an artist's canvas.

**etching** (ET-ching)—Artwork carved on a hard material such as wax that can be used to make multiple prints.

**gallery** (GAL-uh-ree)—A place where artwork is displayed and sold.

**masterpiece** (MAS-tur-peese)—A beautiful or expert piece of artwork.

**musketeer** (mus-keh-TEER)—A soldier who carries a musket, a long-barreled gun fired from the shoulder.

**parable** (PAYR-uh-bul)—A short story that teaches a lesson.

**self-portrait** (self-POR-trut)—A picture that an artist makes of himself or herself.

# Index